German Shepherds

By Kristen Rajczak

 Gareth Stevens
Publishing

Please visit our website, www.garethstevens.com. For a free color catalog of all our high-quality books, call toll free 1-800-542-2595 or fax 1-877-542-2596.

Library of Congress Cataloging-in-Publication Data

Rajczak, Kristen.
German shepherds / Kristen Rajczak.
    p. cm. — (Great big dogs)
Includes index.
ISBN 978-1-4339-5772-7 (pbk.)
ISBN 978-1-4339-5773-4 (6-pack)
ISBN 978-1-4339-5770-3 (library binding)
1. German shepherd dog—Juvenile literature. I. Title.
SF429.G37R35 2011
636.737'6—dc22

                                    2010046047

First Edition

Published in 2012 by
Gareth Stevens Publishing
111 East 14th Street, Suite 349
New York, NY 10003

Designer: Andrea Davison-Bartolotta
Editor: Kristen Rajczak

Photo credits: Cover, p. 1 iStockphoto/Thinkstock; p. 5 Hemera/Thinkstock; pp. 9, 10, 13, 20 Shutterstock.com; p. 6 Fox Photos/Getty Images; p. 14 Andrea Booher/FEMA/Getty Images; p. 17 iStockphoto.com; p. 18 Hulton Archive/Getty Images.

Printed in the United States of America

CPSIA compliance information: Batch #CS11GS: For further information contact Gareth Stevens, New York, New York at 1-800-542-2595.

Contents

Words in the glossary appear in **bold** type the first time they are used in the text.

Top Dog

German shepherds are one of the most popular dog **breeds** in the United States. They may be big, but they are **loyal**, loving pets. A German shepherd likes to be with its family. These large dogs are smart and brave, which makes them good at many different jobs. German shepherds have strong **instincts** and want to guard their home and owners. Because of this, German shepherds make good guard dogs and police dogs.

Dog Tales

There are clubs all over the world for German shepherd lovers!

German shepherds like this one love lots of attention.

Dog Tales

Captain von Stephanitz named his dog Horand.

Since the beginning of the breed, German shepherds have worked well with people.

6

History of the Breed

Farmers in Europe have long used large dogs to do work. They were bred with the skills necessary to herd animals. In the late 1800s, a German army captain, Max von Stephanitz, found a dog that was **related** to these farm dogs. It had features he thought were important: **protective** instincts, cleverness, and strength. With this dog, Captain von Stephanitz started the German shepherd breed. In 1899, he started the Society for the German Shepherd Dog. The American Kennel Club recognized the new breed in 1908.

Coat of Many Colors

German shepherds' coats can be many colors. Some are all black or all white, but most are black and tan. German shepherds have thick outer hair and shorter inner hair. Even with different colors, German shepherds are easy to spot because they have large ears that stand up straight. German shepherds also have a bushy tail that curves up.

German shepherds are usually between 22 and 26 inches (56 and 66 cm) tall at the shoulder and weigh between 75 and 95 pounds (34 and 43 kg).

Dog Tales

Until the 1970s, the German shepherd was called an "Alsatian" in England.

German shepherds' coats can be a combination of many colors.

9

Dog Tales

Dogs who are trained to obey commands do not learn the words. They connect the sound of the command with what they are supposed to do.

German shepherds can be a special part of the family.

▷

Family-Friendly Dogs

German shepherds fit in well with families. They like to please their owners and often show their **affection**. Some people might worry about having such a large dog around children. However, German shepherds treat children like puppies. They are very loving and protective. In fact, German shepherds don't need to be trained as guard dogs—they do it naturally! These dogs have a lot of spirit, though, and must be trained to obey their owners.

On the Job

German shepherds are often used as working dogs. Some are trained to herd or protect animals on a farm. Others guard buildings and people. German shepherds may also work with police officers or the military. They have an excellent sense of smell and can sniff out drugs, bombs, and missing people.

Some German shepherds are used to guide people who do not see or move well. Some even learn to push wheelchairs or open doors!

Dog Tales

German shepherds that work with the military are trained to attack and to patrol the areas in which they work.

This German shepherd went through training to work with the military.

13

This German shepherd will use its sense of smell to find people buried in the fallen building.

German Shepherd Heroes

Many German shepherds help search-and-rescue workers find missing people. These dog heroes may work after a **disaster** like a terrible storm.

A German shepherd named Cassius traveled to the Gulf Coast to help people after Hurricane Katrina in 2005. He and his owner, Peter Taft, found people trapped under buildings that fell. They also went to Haiti after a bad **earthquake** in 2010. Cassius and four other heroic dogs received the 2010 Award for **Canine** Excellence from the American Kennel Club.

Strongheart

Dogs can be movie stars, too! Strongheart was a German shepherd who starred in movies such as *White Fang* during the 1920s. He was a trained police dog who worked with the German military in World War I.

Strongheart was 3 years old when American movie director Laurence Trimble met him. At 125 pounds (57 kg), he was a big dog. Strongheart starred in his first movie, *The Silent Call*, in 1921. He was a great "actor"—they even named a dog food after him!

White Fang is based on a book by Jack London about a dog in the wild.

The Adventures of Rin Tin Tin was first on TV from 1954 to 1959.

18

Rin Tin Tin

Rin Tin Tin was another famous German shepherd. He starred in movies during the 1920s and 1930s. Many later movies and TV shows have featured a dog named Rin Tin Tin, but those German shepherds are not the original Rin Tin Tin. His children and grandchildren took over starring in the many Rin Tin Tin movies and TV shows. They look a lot like the original Rin Tin Tin. Rin Tin Tin's family is one of the oldest in the German shepherd breed.

Owning a German Shepherd

German shepherd owners have companions for many years. In order to stay happy, these dogs need a lot of exercise. Walking and playing helps keep their bodies and brains fit. German shepherds also like to meet other dogs, especially as puppies. Many people choose to take their German shepherds to dog shows. They are great places to show off this beautiful dog!

Learning About German Shepherds

height	22 to 26 inches (56 to 66 cm)
weight	75 to 95 pounds (34 to 43 kg)
coloring	commonly black and tan, but can be white, black, tan, or a mix
life span	10 to 13 years

Glossary

affection: a feeling of love

breed: a group of animals that share features different from other groups of the kind

canine: the group of animals that includes dogs

disaster: an event that causes suffering or loss

earthquake: a shaking or trembling of the earth because of movement underground

instinct: a natural ability

loyal: faithful

protective: concerned with keeping someone or something safe

related: connected by family

For More Information

Books

Rappaport, Jill. *Jack & Jill: The Miracle Dog with a Happy Tail to Tell.* New York, NY: Collins, 2009.

Schuh, Mari C. *German Shepherds.* Minneapolis, MN: Bellwether Media, 2009.

Websites

The German Shepherd Dog Club of America
www.gsdca.org
Learn more about owning, caring for, and showing German shepherds.

Rin Tin Tin
www.rintintin.com
Find out more about this movie-star dog. Read the story of Rin Tin Tin and see if he is coming to visit a town near you.

Index